HUEY P. LONG
Talker and Doer

HUEY P. LONG
Talker and Doer

Written by David R. Collins

Illustrated by
Jack K. Smith

PELICAN PUBLISHING COMPANY
Gretna 2003

*The word "Pelican" and the depiction of a pelican are trademarks
of Pelican Publishing Company, Inc., and are registered
in the U.S. Patent and Trademark Office.*

Library of Congress Cataloging-in-Publication Data

Collins, David R.
    Huey P. Long : talker and doer / written by David R. Collins ; illustrated by Jack K Smith.
      p. cm.
    ISBN 1-56554-913-9 (alk. paper)
    1. Long, Huey Pierce, 1893-1935—Juvenile literature. 2. Legislators—United States—Biography—Juvenile literature. 3. United States. Congress. Senate—Biography—Juvenile literature. 4. Governors—Louisiana—Biography—Juvenile literature. 5. Louisiana—Politics and government—1865-1950—Juvenile literature. [1. Long, Huey Pierce, 1893-1935. 2. Governors. 3. Louisiana—Politics and government—1865-1950.] I. Smith, Jack K., ill. II. Title.

E748.L86 C65 2003
976.3'062'092—dc21
[B]
                                                         2002013496

Printed in China
Published by Pelican Publishing Company, Inc.
1000 Burmaster Street, Gretna, Louisiana 70053

HUEY P. LONG: TALKER AND DOER

Huey P. Long, Jr., was a talker. "He came into the world talking," said his father, "and he never did quiet down." Huey was born on August 30, 1893, near Winnfield, Louisiana.

Huey had eight brothers and sisters. They all played hide-and-seek on the family farm. Huey loved climbing big trees and hiding in branches.

In school Huey was bored. He squirmed and talked to his classmates.

"Maybe *you* could teach this lesson better," one teacher said.

"I'm sure I could," Huey answered with a smile.

One thing Huey *did* like about school was debate. He liked to find information and give speeches. His voice was clear and loud.

"You sure know how to talk," his classmates said.

At seventeen, Huey went to work selling cooking oil. "I can sell anything to anybody," he bragged. Huey traveled from door to door and town to town. People bought his cooking oil whether they needed it or not.

In Shreveport, Louisiana, Huey held a contest. He asked people to bake pies and cakes using his cooking oil. A girl named Rose McConnell won. After that, Huey and Rose took long walks and went on picnics. They were married in 1913.

Huey had big plans. He dreamed of becoming governor, senator, even president of the United States! But first he wanted to study law.

Huey went to Tulane Law School in New Orleans. Soon he ran out of money. Huey convinced his teachers to give him a big law test. He passed the test with top grades, getting his law degree in one year instead of three!

In 1915 Huey and Rose headed back to Winnfield. There were many poor people there—people Huey wanted to help. He helped people whether they could pay or not.

At twenty-four, Huey was too young to run for governor, senator, or president. But he *could* run for railroad commissioner. He did just that, and he won!

Companies tried to raise taxes. "Oh, no, you don't!" said Huey. He gave speeches in the United States Supreme Court. "The rich get rich and the poor get poorer," Huey told the judges. They voted on his side.

As soon as he was old enough, Huey P. Long ran for governor. He rode around Louisiana in a beat-up car. He talked to big groups and small groups. But he lost the election. "I'll be back," he promised.

Huey kept his word in 1928. From morning to night he talked to people and they listened. This time Huey won.

Louisiana needed better roads. It needed more bridges and good hospitals. As governor, Huey got them all built. He even built a brand-new capitol building, the tallest building in the South!

Huey solved another big problem. Poor people could not afford to rent schoolbooks for their children, and many of their kids dropped out of school. "Boys and girls should have *free* schoolbooks," Huey said. He got laws passed so that every child in Louisiana would have free schoolbooks. It was the first state in the country to provide free textbooks for students.

Some people did not like Huey. They said he was too bossy. They said he helped out his friends and took money from the government.

Huey shook his head. "Prove it!" he said.

No one could.

Sometimes Huey wore white suits and orange suits when he gave speeches. His face turned red like a tomato. "He looks like a clown," some people said. "He sure doesn't talk like one," others answered.

Huey liked to listen to the radio. His favorite character was the Kingfish. The Kingfish liked to talk a lot and try to fool people. Huey called himself "The Kingfish."

Huey wanted everyone to feel important. "Every man a king," he said. People cheered when he said that. They cheered louder when he said, "But no one wears a crown."

Huey and Rose had three children—Rose, Russell, and Palmer. They did not get to see their father often. He spent lots of time traveling and giving speeches. But birthdays and holidays were special family times. Huey always had new stories and jokes to share with his family.

The Louisiana State University football team in Baton Rouge was like his family too. Huey went to lots of games. He sat with the team on the bench. No one cheered louder than Huey. He hired a leader for the band. Huey even helped write the school fight song.

In 1930, the Louisiana voters elected Huey P. Long, Jr., as a senator. He packed his bags and headed off to Washington, D.C.

Huey suggested that all people "share the wealth" of the country. Share the Wealth Clubs sprang up. "Huey P. Long would make a good president," people said. Letters from Louisiana flooded his office. Many called Huey "Mr. Louisiana."

MR. LOUISIANA
LONG FOR PRESIDENT
HUEY P. LONG
Long
SHARE THE WEALTH

During the summer of 1935 Huey came back to Louisiana. He went to see his friends in the Capitol Building in Baton Rouge. Suddenly a man stepped forward and fired a gun. Huey was shot. The Capitol guards fired their guns at the man who had shot Huey. The man fell to the ground, dead. Huey stumbled a ways, then collapsed. "Who would shoot me?" he asked.

The answer was a dentist named Carl Weiss. He was angry at Huey for saying bad things about his family. On September 10, 1935, Huey P. Long, Jr., died.

Huey left Louisiana with paved roads and bridges where none existed before. He left Louisiana with a fine medical school, training doctors and nurses to serve the people of the state and beyond. He left Louisiana with a charity hospital system, where poor people could go for free medical care. He left public schools with free textbooks for all. And he left a strong state university where poor students could attend at low cost. He was quite a talker. But he was quite a "doer" too.